HAPPY GOODIES

FREE DIGITAL COLORING PAGES

Thank you for choosing our book!

To access your free digital print coloring pages scan the Qr Code below!

scan me :)
for more fun!

HAPPY GOODIES

Before you start coloring!

it's recommended to utilize Amazon's paper selection,
which is best suited for colored pencils and alcohol-based markers.
If you plan to use wet mediums, it's suggested to place
a sheet of paper behind the page you're coloring to prevent
any potential bleed-through.

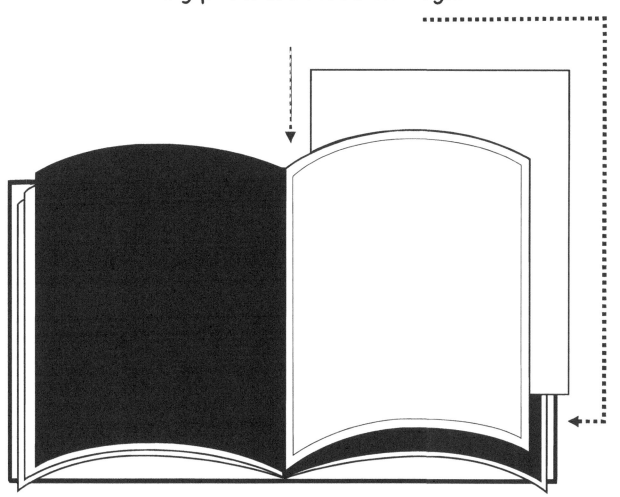

Enjoy coloring!

HAPPY
GOODIES

Coloring Test Page

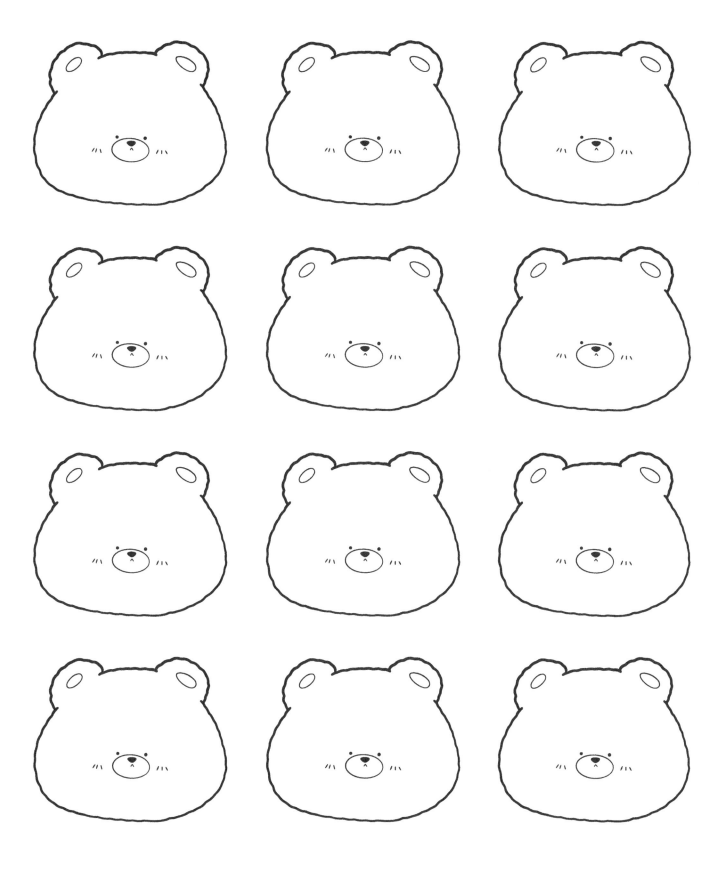

HAPPY
GOODIES

THIS BOOK BELONGS TO:

HAPPY
GOODIES

Coloring check list:

❀Making ❀Video Game Day ❀Taking photos together
macaroons ❀Hot springs ❀Diving
❀Donut Day ❀Breakfast toast ❀The ice cream truck is
❀We're flying! ❀Beach vacation here!
❀Fun at the ❀Toy machine ❀Fun on the river
store ❀Picnic
❀At home ❀Breakfast with a ❀Happy Birthday!
❀Christmas friend ❀Skiing down the mountain
❀Drawing ❀TV day ❀Sorting out clothes
❀Karaoke ❀Watching movies ❀Summer day
together ❀A trip on the subway
❀Beach volleyball ❀Evening out
❀Flower Drive ❀Getting ready for
bedtime

HAPPY
GOODIES

Making Macaroons

HAPPY GOODIES

Donut Day

HAPPY
GOODIES

We're flying!

HAPPY GOODIES

Fun At The Store

HAPPY
GOODIES

At Home

HAPPY
GOODIES

HAPPY
GOODIES

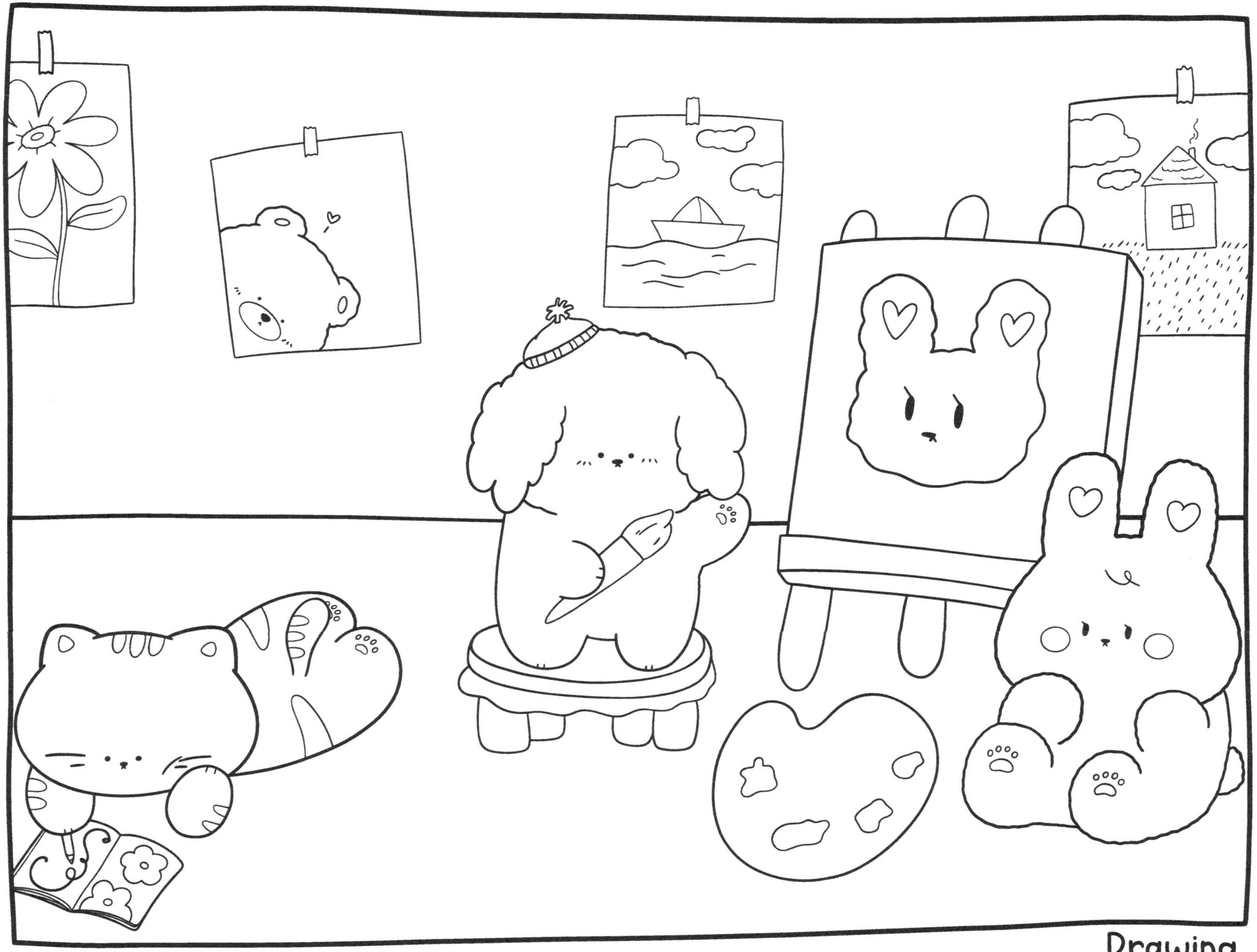

Drawing

HAPPY
GOODIES

Karaoke

HAPPY GOODIES

Beach Volleyball

HAPPY
GOODIES

Flower Drive

HAPPY
GOODIES

Video Game Day

HAPPY GOODIES

Hot Springs

HAPPY
GOODIES

Breakfast Toast

HAPPY
GOODIES

Beach Vacation

HAPPY
GOODIES

Toy Machine

HAPPY
GOODIES

Breakfast With A Friend

HAPPY
GOODIES

Tv Day

HAPPY
GOODIES

Watching Movies Together

HAPPY GOODIES

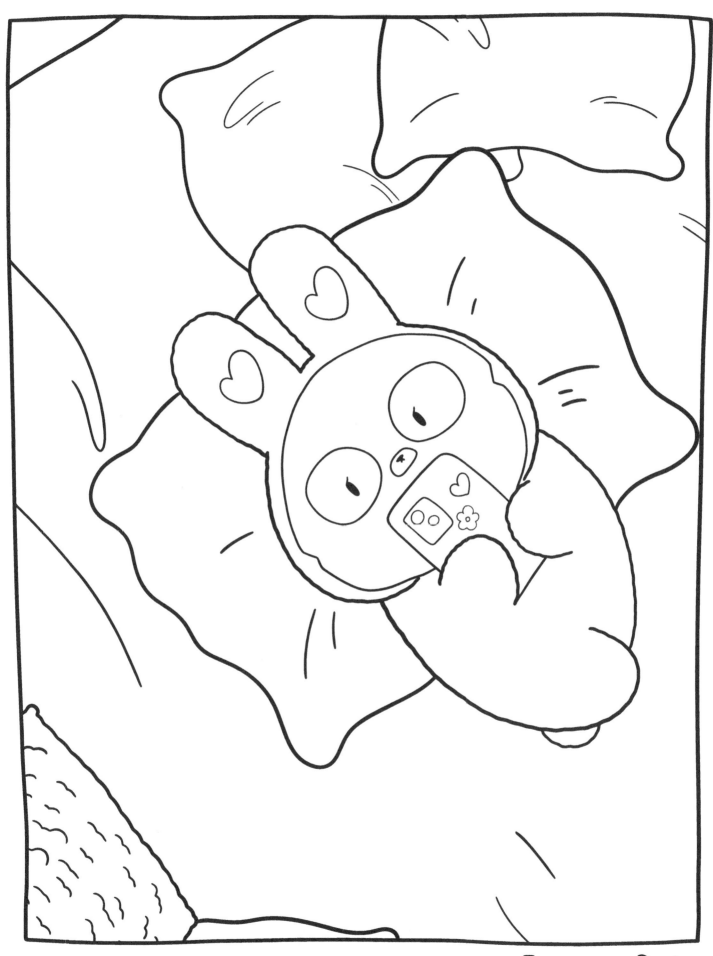

Evening Out

HAPPY
GOODIES

Getting Ready For Bedtime

HAPPY GOODIES

Taking Photos Together

HAPPY
GOODIES

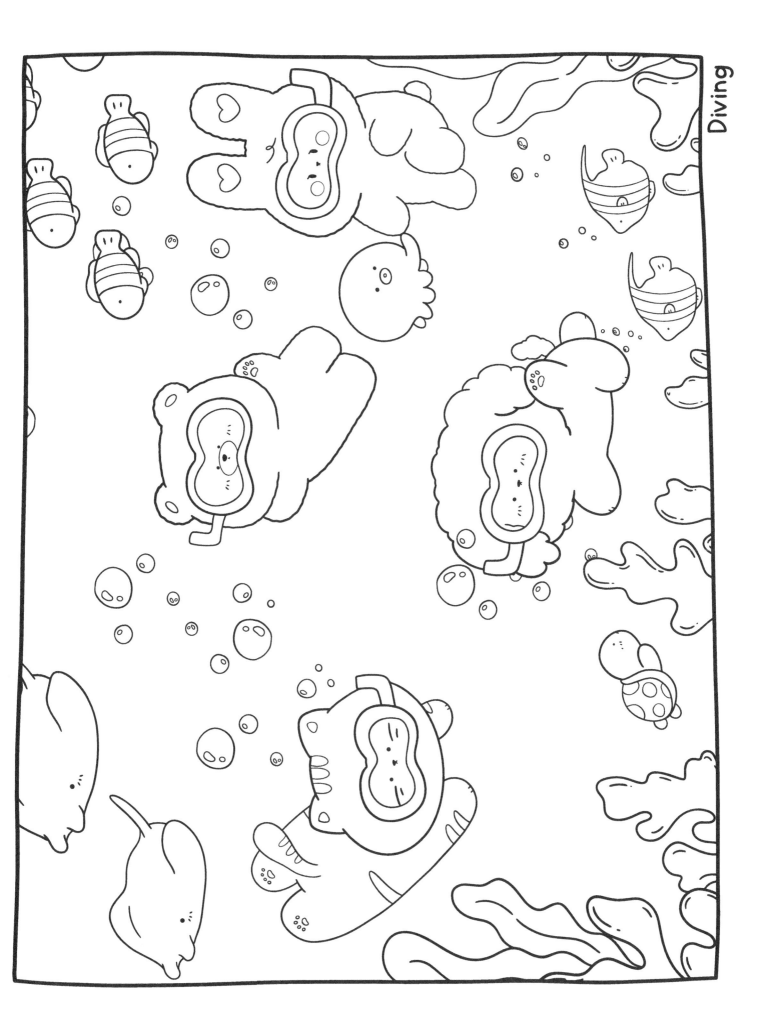

HAPPY GOODIES

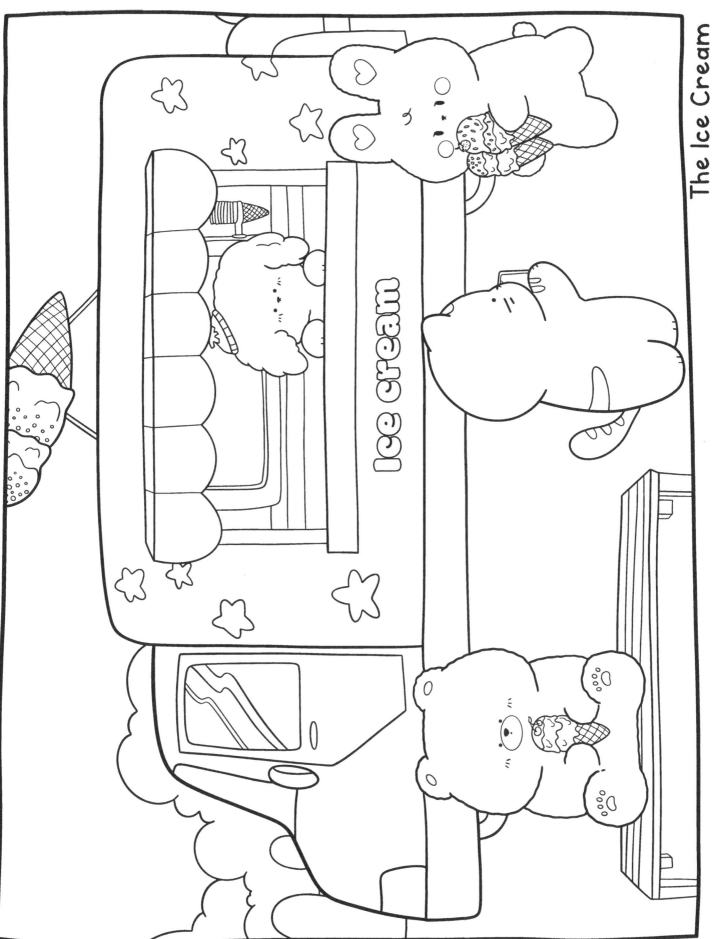

HAPPY
GOODIES

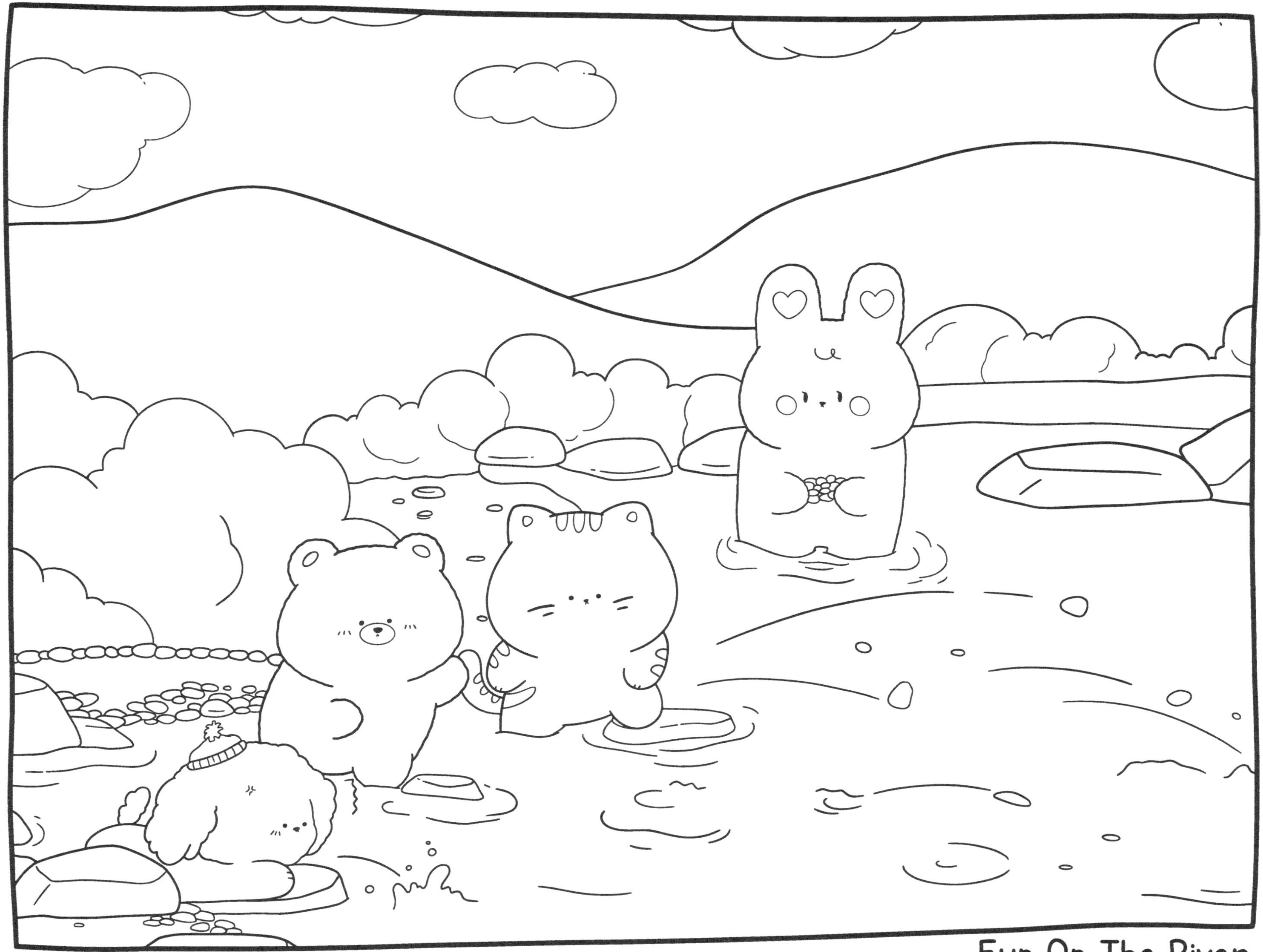

Fun On The River

HAPPY GOODIES

HAPPY
GOODIES

Happy Bday

HAPPY GOODIES

Skiing Down The Mountain

HAPPY
GOODIES

Sorting Out Clothes

HAPPY
GOODIES

HAPPY
GOODIES

A Trip on The Subway

HAPPY
GOODIES

Thank you!!

Wow! You've reached the end of our coloring adventure! We're so grateful that you joined us on this journey of creativity and fun.

We hope you colored your heart out and unleashed your inner artist. Every page you colored became a unique masterpiece!

Feeling proud of your creations? Share them with the world! Snap a picture and share it with us on social media!

scan the Qr code and follow us there!

scan me :) for more fun!

HAPPY GOODIES

Made in the USA
Las Vegas, NV
22 April 2024

89007633R00044